A Crabtree Branches Book
Today's Stars
TAYLOR SWIFT
I0813153
Ellen Rodger
Crabtree Publishing
crabtreebooks.com

School-to-Home Support for Caregivers and Teachers

This high-interest book is designed to motivate striving students with engaging topics while building fluency, vocabulary, and an interest in reading. Here are a few questions and activities to help the reader build upon his or her comprehension skills.

Before Reading:

- *What do I think this book is about?*
- *What do I know about this topic?*
- *What do I want to learn about this topic?*
- *Why am I reading this book?*

During Reading:

- *I wonder why...*
- *I'm curious to know...*
- *How is this like something I already know?*
- *What have I learned so far?*

After Reading:

- *What was the author trying to teach me?*
- *What are some details?*
- *How did the photographs and captions help me understand more?*
- *Read the book again and look for the vocabulary words.*
- *What questions do I still have?*

Extension Activities:

- *What was your favorite part of the book? Write a paragraph on it.*
- *Draw a picture of your favorite thing you learned from the book.*

TABLE OF CONTENTS

World's Biggest Pop Star 4

First Love: Country 8

Rising Artist 12

Pop Music Leap 16

Branching Out 20

All the Love 24

Glossary 30

Index 31

Websites to Visit 31

About the Author 32

WORLD'S BIGGEST POP STAR

Taylor Swift has been called the world's biggest pop star. She has won many awards, including four **Grammy** Album of the Year awards. That's the most won by any artist! Taylor is also a major **influencer**. She encourages her massive fan base to be kind to each other and to support causes that help people.

Taylor Swift is one of the world's best-selling music artists.

Taylor Alison Swift was born on December 13, 1989, in West Reading, Pennsylvania. Her parents, Scott and Andrea, named her Taylor after American singer-songwriter James Taylor. Taylor grew up on her family's Christmas tree farm.

Taylor's parents recognized her musical talents from a young age and have supported her throughout her career.

Fun Facts

Taylor Swift's **devoted** fans are called Swifties. Taylor is proud of her fans. Swifties often share handmade beaded bracelets with each other when at Taylor's concerts or events.

FIRST LOVE: COUNTRY

As a young child, Taylor sang in church. She also took singing and acting lessons. Taylor progressed into musical theater in school, but her first love was country music.

At age 11, Taylor and her mother traveled to Nashville to deliver **demo tapes** she had recorded to record labels. The labels rejected Taylor's early efforts. But she did not let that stop her. Instead, Taylor focused on learning how to play guitar and write her own music.

Nashville, Tennessee, is known for its vibrant music scene, earning it the nickname "Music City."

When she was 13, Taylor sang “The Star Spangled Banner” at the U.S. Open Tennis Championship. That performance got her noticed. Soon, Taylor had a manager. She recorded a demo where she performed her own songs. A record deal followed.

*Taylor learned to feel comfortable with an audience by doing **karaoke** and entering singing competitions.*

Fun Facts

Taylor's family moved to Hendersonville, Tennessee, which is close to Nashville, so that she could work in the home of country music! She went to high school in Hendersonville.

RISING ARTIST

When her record label, RCA, insisted she record other people's songs, Taylor decided to leave. She signed a **contract** with Sony/ATV Publishing to write music. She was just 14 years old!

While she was writing, Taylor was also performing at Nashville music venues. At a Bluebird Cafe performance in 2005, a music industry representative spotted her. He signed her to record an album of her own music.

The Bluebird Cafe gives songwriters a chance to perform their work. Many famous music artists have got their start there.

Taylor's first album, *Taylor Swift*, was released in October 2006. It had two number-one hits. The album made Taylor a country music star and put her in the record books. Soon, she launched her first tour.

Taylor considers 13 to be her lucky number. She has featured it in her songs and painted it on her hand before shows.

Fun Facts

At 16 years old, Taylor's first album earned her a Country Music Association (CMA) award for Best New Artist. Taylor also received a Favorite Country Female Artist award from the American Music Awards.

POP MUSIC LEAP

Taylor experimented with a more pop music sound with the release of her second album, *Fearless*, in 2008. It went on to win several music awards, including a Grammy for Album of the Year.

Taylor's song "You Belong With Me" topped the music charts in all **genres**. She headlined a 118-date concert tour for the album.

Taylor became the youngest person to be named Entertainer of the Year at the CMA Awards in 2009.

While fame and **acclaim** at such a young age wasn't always easy, Taylor proved herself to be strong and independent. At the 2009 MTV Video Music Awards (VMAs), Taylor was interrupted by rapper Kanye West during an acceptance speech. Kanye felt the award should go to the artist Beyoncé. As he talked over her, Taylor stayed calm and respectful.

Taylor won her first VMA for Best Female Video for "You Belong With Me."

Fun Facts

Later at the same VMAs, Beyoncé was awarded Video of the Year. She invited Taylor onstage to finish the speech Kanye interrupted. The crowd went wild for both performers.

BRANCHING OUT

Taylor's fame and recognition brought her acting roles. She has appeared in several films and television shows. She has also written and performed songs for numerous films.

Taylor voiced the character of Audrey in the 2012 animated movie The Lorax.

Fun Facts

Fans have many nicknames for Taylor, including Tay, T-Swizzle, and Tay Tay.

As one of the most influential artists in the world, Taylor has a lot to say about things that are important to her. Most often, she makes those statements in her songs. Since her first album in 2006, she has released 14 more.

Taylor has won 14 Grammys and been nominated for 58.

Some of Taylor's albums are re-recordings of earlier albums. She lost control of the original recordings when they were purchased by a music **producer**. Unable to get them back, Taylor decided to remake them. These albums are called "Taylor's Version."

Taylor believes artists should own their own work.

ALL THE LOVE

Fans of Taylor Swift are devoted to their favorite artist. They love how she sings about her relationships with friends and boyfriends. Taylor loves her fans back. She follows fans online, and invites them into her life. She encourages them to believe in themselves.

Taylor puts on massive concert tours throughout the world to reach her fans.

As one of the most powerful pop stars in the world, Taylor has made a lot of money. She appreciates her wealth and **privilege** and honors it by giving back to others.

Taylor Swift concerts bring in lots of money to the cities where she plays. One album concert tour is thought to earn close to $5 billion for the U.S. economy alone.

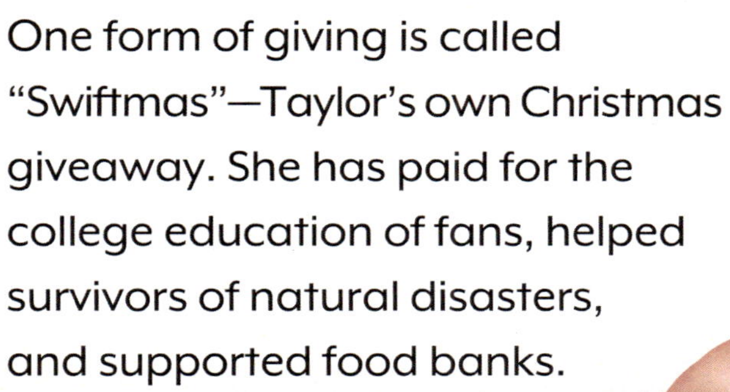

One form of giving is called "Swiftmas"—Taylor's own Christmas giveaway. She has paid for the college education of fans, helped survivors of natural disasters, and supported food banks.

Taylor donated $4 million to build an education center at the Country Music Hall of Fame and Museum in Nashville.

Taylor Swift has the ability to reach people with her music. Swifties love her dedication to friendship. Music lovers point out her ability to write honestly about relationships.

Swifties are friendly to each other.
They are from all age groups and backgrounds.

Taylor's skills in re-inventing herself make her really appealing to fans. She isn't afraid to show her emotions and helps others do the same.

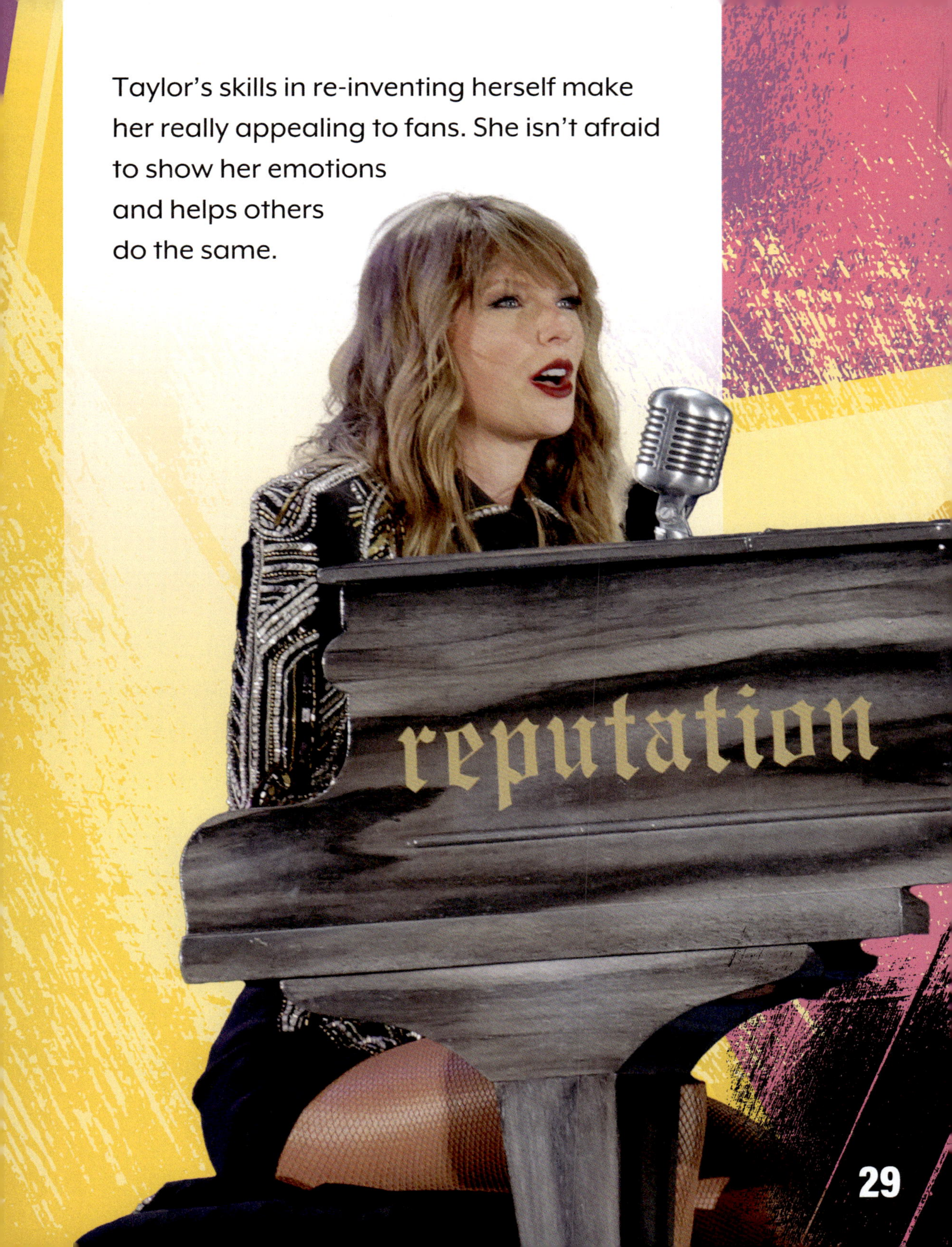

GLOSSARY

acclaim (uh-KLEYM): Enthusiastic approval or praise

contract (KON-trakt): A legal agreement between two or more people

demo tapes (DEM-oh teyps): Recordings of songs by an unknown singer that are distributed to record companies to show the skills and talents of the performer

devoted (dih-VOH-tid): Loyal and firm attachment or affection for someone

genres (ZHAHN-ruhs): Types or categories of music

Grammy (GRAM-ee): An award given by the Recording Academy of the United States to recognize an outstanding achievement in music

influencer (IN-floo-unh-ser): A person who has the power to influence people, or has an effect on their thoughts, opinions, or actions

karaoke (kar-ee-OH-kee): A form of entertainment where people sing along to a music video for which the original vocals have been removed

privilege (PRIV-uh-lij): Enjoying special rights and advantages

producer (pruh-DOO-ser): A person who oversees the making of a music recording

INDEX

acting 8, 20

albums 4, 13, 14, 15, 16, 17, 22, 23

awards 4, 15, 16, 17, 18, 19

causes 4, 26–27

concerts 7, 17, 25, 26

family 6, 9, 11

influencer 4, 22

Nashville 9, 11, 13, 27

songwriting 6, 9, 12, 13, 22, 28

Swifties 7, 28

WEBSITES TO VISIT

https://kids.britannica.com/students/article/Taylor-Swift/487625

https://theswiftmuseum.com

https://www.grammy.com/artists/taylor-swift/15450

ABOUT THE AUTHOR

Ellen Rodger won a bank-sponsored short story contest at age nine. It was the last thing her bank ever gave her for free, but it kicked-started a career in newspaper, magazine, and book publishing. Ellen has written hundreds of books for curious young people, on topics as varied as the history of the potato, urban wildlife, refugees, the Great Lakes, and explorers.

Crabtree Publishing

crabtreebooks.com   800-387-7650

Written by: Ellen Rodger
Designed by: Kathy Walsh
Series Development: James Earley
Editor: Melissa Boyce
Educational Consultant: Marie Lemke M.Ed.
Production manager: Candice Campbell

Hardcover: 978-1-0398-8034-4
Paperback: 978-1-0398-8394-9
Ebook (pdf): 978-1-0398-8154-9
Epub: 978-1-0398-8274-4

Printed in the U.S.A./CP2025

Published in Canada
Crabtree Publishing
616 Welland Ave.
St. Catharines, Ontario
L2M 5V6

Published in the United States
Crabtree Publishing
347 Fifth Ave
Suite 1402-145
New York, NY 10016

Library and Archives Canada Cataloguing in Publication
Available at Library and Archives Canada

Library of Congress Cataloging-in-Publication Data
Available at the Library of Congress

Photographs
Alamy: WENN p 6, 19, Cinematic Collection p 20
Newscom: TERRY WYATT p 17
Shutterstock: Brian Friedman, cover, title page; Tinseltown, TOC; Scott Prokop, p 4, p 26; s_bukley, p 5, 9 15; Graham Drew Photography, p 7 (top), p 24 (left), p 28; Everett Collection, p 8, p 12, p 16; Photo Spirit, p 9; MILA PARH, p 11 (top); Dee Browning, p 13; Brian Friedman, p 21; Free, p 22, p 27 (right); ChristinaAiko Photography, p 23; ezellhphotography, p 24 (right), p 25 (top); Christian Bertrand, p 25 (bottom); melissamn, p 27 (left); Featureflash Photo Agency, p 32
Wikimedia: Creative Commons, p 10, p 11 (bottom), p 14, p 18; Ronald Woan, p 29
All other images from Shutterstock